Guidebook for

NORTH CAROLINA

Property
Mappers

William A. Campbell

Guidebook for

NORTH CAROLINA

Property
Mappers

Third Edition

2001

ESTABLISHED IN 1931, the Institute of Government provides training, advisory, and research services to public officials and others interested in the operation of state and local government in North Carolina. A part of The University of North Carolina at Chapel Hill, the Institute also administers the university's Master of Public Administration Program.

Each year approximately 14,000 city, county, and state officials attend one or more of the 230 classes, seminars, and conferences offered by the Institute. Faculty members annually publish up to fifty books, bulletins, and other reference works related to state and local government. Each day that the General Assembly is in session, the Institute's *Daily Bulletin*, available in print and electronically, reports on the day's activities for members of the legislature and others who need to follow the course of legislation. An extensive Web site (http://ncinfo.iog.unc.edu/) provides access to publications and faculty research, course listings, program and service information, and links to other useful sites related to government.

Support for the Institute's operations comes from various sources, including state appropriations, local government membership dues, private contributions, publication sales, and service contracts. For more information about the Institute, visit the Web site or call (919) 966-5381.

Michael R. Smith, DIRECTOR
Thomas H. Thornburg, ASSOCIATE DIRECTOR FOR PROGRAMS
Patricia A. Langelier, ASSOCIATE DIRECTOR FOR PLANNING AND OPERATIONS
Ann C. Simpson, ASSOCIATE DIRECTOR FOR DEVELOPMENT

FACULTY

Gregory S. Allison
Stephen Allred
David N. Ammons
A. Fleming Bell, II
Maureen M. Berner
Frayda S. Bluestein
Mark F. Botts
Phillip Boyle
Joan G. Brannon
Anita R. Brown-Graham
  (on leave)
William A. Campbell
Stevens H. Clarke
Anne S. Davidson

Anne M. Dellinger
James C. Drennan
Richard D. Ducker
Robert L. Farb
Joseph S. Ferrell
Susan Leigh Flinspach
Kimberly Martin Grantham
Milton S. Heath, Jr.
Cheryl Daniels Howell
Joseph E. Hunt
Kurt J. Jenne
Robert P. Joyce
David M. Lawrence
Charles D. Liner

Ben F. Loeb, Jr.
Janet Mason
Laurie L. Mesibov
Jill D. Moore
David W. Owens
William C. Rivenbark
John Rubin
John L. Saxon
Jessica Smith
John B. Stephens
A. John Vogt
Richard Whisnant
Gordon P. Whitaker
Warren Jake Wicker

© 1995, 1998, 2001
INSTITUTE OF GOVERNMENT
CB#3330, Knapp Building
The University of North Carolina at Chapel Hill
Chapel Hill, NC 27599-3330

Printed in the United States of America

21 20 19 18 17   5 6 7 8 9

ISBN 978-1-56011-391-1

Preface

This *Guidebook for North Carolina Property Mappers* is intended to aid property mappers, review officers, land records managers, and county assessors in their work. Other local government officials who handle real estate transactions or deal with land records may find the book useful, but it is written for property mappers, and I have tried to keep their questions and needs in mind. Chapter I is an introduction to real property law; Chapter II describes how to find and use various property records; Chapter III deals with listing property and determining ownership for purposes of the ad valorem property tax; and Chapter IV discusses the duties of review officers in certifying maps for recording.

This third edition of the *Guidebook* is made necessary by the numerous changes in the law and procedures that have occurred during the six years since the second edition was published in 1995. In particular, this new edition contains a chapter dealing with the responsibilities of review officers, many of whom are property mappers.

William A. Campbell
Spring 2001

Contents

Guidebook for

Property Mappers

I. Real Property Law

§ 100. Real Property Defined

Property is divided into two categories, real and personal. Real property includes land, buildings, and other improvements permanently attached to the land.[1] Minerals under the surface of the land or imbedded in the surface are real property[2] as is standing timber.[3] Cultivated crops, however, are treated as personal property.[4] For property tax purposes the North Carolina Machinery Act summarizes the common law definition by providing that "real property . . . mean[s] not only the land itself, but also buildings, structures, improvements, and permanent fixtures thereon, and all rights and privileges belonging or in any wise appertaining thereto."[5]

Fixtures are sometimes treated as real property and sometimes as personal property. A fixture is an item of property that in its original form was personal property but has become attached to real property.[6] For example, a manufactured brick and a door at the lumberyard are personal property, but when they become part of a house they are real property. Whether or not personal property affixed to land is a fixture depends on whether the person who put it there intended for it to remain permanently. As evidence of that intention, courts ask whether there was an agreement concerning removal of the property, how easily the building or other improvement can be removed from the land without causing structural damage, and whether the owner of the improvement also owns the land on which it is situated.[7] If the owner of the personal property has an agreement with the owner of the land that the property is to be removed at some time in the future—as is usually the case with business or "trade" fixtures—the personal property does not become a fixture and is always treated as personal property. If, however, there is no agreement concerning removal, or the property cannot be easily separated from the land, or the owner of the personal property also owns the land, then there is evidence that the owner intended for the personal property to become a fixture.

Mobile homes are sometimes classified as real property and sometimes as personal property for property tax purposes. The circumstances of each case will dictate how the mobile home is to be classified, but as a general matter, if the mobile home is in a mobile home park or on other property owned by someone other than the owner of the home, it should be treated as personal property. If it is on land owned by the owner of the mobile home and is on a foundation or is improved by the addition of a porch, carport, or room, it may be treated as real property. G.S. 105-273(13) requires a mobile home to be classified as real property for property tax purposes if it (1) was constructed in two or more sections; (2) has the moving hitch, wheels, and axles removed; (3) is placed on a permanent enclosed foundation; and (4) is on land owned by the owner of the mobile home.

§ 101. Estates in Land

Introduction

The estate that a person has in land is the group of rights he or she holds regarding that land and the duration of ownership.[8] The law regarding estates has been shaped into its present form by statutory changes and American judicial decisions, but its foundations are in ancient English land law,[9] and this history accounts for some of its current principles and most of its terminology. The estates discussed here are the fee simple, the fee simple determinable, the fee simple subject to a condition subsequent, and the life estate. Although leasehold interests are sometimes treated as estates in land,[10] they are largely governed by principles of contract law[11] and by statute,[12] and in any event are of little interest to property mappers.

Fee Simple

The estate that gives the owner the largest group of rights is the fee simple, sometimes called "fee simple absolute." The owner of land in fee simple is able to use the land for any purpose he or she sees fit, within the scope of zoning and other land-use restrictions, and is able to transfer it by deed during his or her life and by will at death to any person.[13]

An important qualification on this right of transferability is that if a husband or wife who owns property in fee simple in his or her own name transfers it by deed, the other spouse must sign the deed to release his or her statutory dower right.[14] This right gives a surviving spouse whose wife or husband died without a will, or who dissents from the will, a life estate in one third of all the real property the deceased spouse owned during the marriage.[15] Thus it is most important that the other spouse join in the conveyance if the grantee is to obtain a good title. This is why property mappers frequently see deeds in which both husband and wife sign as grantors even though the property is owned by only one of them and not as tenants by the entireties (discussed in Section 103). This is also why mappers sometimes see in deeds the name of an unmarried grantor followed by such terms as "widower" in the case of a man and "widow" or "feme sole" in the case of a woman. These designations indicate to anyone examining the deed that there was no spouse who should have joined in the conveyance.

Fee Simple Determinable

A fee simple determinable contains language in the deed or will creating it that automatically terminates the estate if a certain event occurs.[16] The event may never occur, in which case the owner of the land is in the same position as though a fee simple absolute were held. An example of language that creates a fee simple determinable is, "To the trustees of the First Presbyterian Church so long as the land is used for church purposes, but when it is no longer so used it shall revert to [the grantor] and his heirs." If the stated event occurs (the church sells the property to a drive-in restaurant), the property automatically reverts to the grantor or his heirs. The significant element in language creating a fee simple determinable, and what distinguishes it from a fee simple conditional, is that the estate terminates automatically upon the happening of the event; no one has to take any further action.

Fee Simple Subject to a Condition Subsequent

A fee simple subject to a condition subsequent is similar to a fee simple determinable in that the language of the granting instrument states that the grantee or devisee will be divested of the property if a certain event occurs. But it is different in that the divestment is not automatic; instead, the grantors or their heirs must act to displace the holder of the estate.[17] Typical language creating a fee simple subject to a condition subsequent is, "To the First Presbyterian Church on the condition that the property is used for church purposes, but if it is no longer used as a church this deed shall be void." In this instance the church does not automatically forfeit its title when it sells the property to the Jiffy Mart; rather, the grantor or his or her heirs must take legal action to enforce the condition and accomplish the divestment.

Termination of Rights of Reverter and Entry

A person who may receive title to real property in the event a fee simple determinable ends has what is known as a possibility of reverter. A person who may attempt to recover the title to real property when the estate is a fee simple subject to a condition subsequent has what is known as a right of entry. By statute,[18] North Carolina has limited the life of these interests to a period of sixty years, if the interest was created after October 1, 1995. This means, for example, that if a fee simple determinable is created after October 1, 1995, and it does not revert—does not vest in the person holding the possiblity of reverter—within sixty years from the date of its creation, it is void, and the title becomes one in fee simple absolute. This sixty-year limitation does not apply if the possibility of reverter or right of entry is held by a charity or government agency.

Life Estate

A life estate is an estate with most of the attributes of a fee simple except that it terminates at the death of the life tenant or other named person.[19] Typical language creating a life estate is "To B, for his life." If the deed or will does not name a person to whom the property is to go at the death of the life tenant, a reversion is created, and the property reverts to the grantor or his or her heirs.[20] If the grantor names another person to receive the property at the death of the life tenant by such language as "To B, for life, and then to C," a remainder interest has been given to C, who is called the remainderman.[21] A life tenant may sell the life estate,[22] but the estate will still revert or go to a remainderman at the death of the life tenant. Although property mappers may occasionally see a life estate created in a deed, they are more likely to see one in a will, for it is a popular estate-planning device.

§ 102. Easements

Definition

An easement is a right to use or restrict the use of another person's land; it is not an estate in land.[23] Easements are usually classified as in gross or appurtenant and affirmative or negative.[24]

Easement in Gross

An easement in gross is a right personal to the holder and is not for the benefit of another tract of land.[25] It is extinguished at the death of the owner and is not assignable.[26] Although the extinguishability of easements in gross should be of concern to private individuals, it is generally not of concern to government agencies and corporations, which hold many easements in gross such as utility easements and bicycle and trail easements.

Easement Appurtenant

An easement appurtenant is an easement on one parcel of land that benefits another parcel.[27] For example, if A and B are adjoining parcels of land and the owner of parcel A grants the owner of B a road easement across A, the easement is appurtenant. The parcel subject to the easement is the servient tract; the parcel benefited is the dominant tract. An appurtenant easement attaches to and passes with the dominant tract as an interest in real property.[28]

Affirmative Easement

An affirmative easement empowers the holder to go on the land subject to the easement or to place structures on it.[29] Examples of affirmative easements are utility easements, road easements, and sidewalk easements.

Negative Easement

A negative easement empowers the holder to restrict the use of the land subject to the easement but does not empower the holder to go on the land or place any structure on the land.[30] An example of a negative easement is a conservation easement, which may restrict building, removal of vegetation, and other activities on the land protected by the easement.[31]

Creation

Easements may be created in a number of ways.[32] Most easements are created by grant, reservation, or dedication. In a grant the owner of the servient tract executes a document similar to a deed and gives the easement rights to another person.[33] In a reservation a landowner who sells one tract and retains another reserves an easement in the conveyed tract by language in the deed to that tract.[34] In a dedication a landowner grants certain rights to the public in the land, typically in the form of street rights-of-way.[35] Before an easement by dedication is created, the landowner must make an offer of dedication and a public agency must accept the offer.[36] Most offers of dedication today are made expressly by showing the dedicated streets on a subdivision plat that is submitted for approval,[37] but the offer of dedication can also be found to have been made presumptively by, for example, the sale of lots by reference to a subdivision plat that shows streets and roads.[38] Acceptance of the offer of dedication can be made formally by adoption of a resolution,[39] or it can be by other than formal means, such as by exercising control over the streets offered for dedication and maintaining them.[40]

Railroad Rights-of-Way

Property mappers may occasionally encounter mapping problems where railroad rights-of-way have been abandoned. In this regard it is important to note that although the term "right-of-way" is often considered to mean an easement,[41] railroads in North Carolina acquired rights-of-way in fee simple as well as by easement. G.S. 1-44.1 provides that when the tracks have been removed and no railroad activity has been conducted on the property for seven years, the railroad is presumed to have abandoned the right-of-way. This presumption, however, applies only when the right-of-way was an easement and not to fee simple ownership.[42] G.S. 1-44.2 in turn provides that when a railroad abandons part of its right-of-way, title to the abandoned property is presumed to be vested in the adjacent landowners, with the presumptive ownership extending to the centerline of the abandoned easement.

If the abandoned easement adjoins a public road, the adjacent property owner's right of ownership extends to the nearest edge of the road right-of-way. In *Nelson v. Battle Forest Friends Meeting*,[43] a public road ran parallel to an abandoned railroad easement but lay wholly within the limits of the 100-foot railroad easement. The plaintiff, an adjacent landowner, claimed title to the centerline of the abandoned easement. The defendant, the other adjacent landowner, relying on G.S. 1-44.2(a), contended that the plaintiff's title extended only to the edge of the road. The North Carolina Supreme Court held that G.S. 1-44.2(a) did not apply to limit the plaintiff's title because the abandoned easement did not *adjoin* the public road. The court said that because the road was wholly within the bounds of the easement, it could not adjoin the easement. The court held that the plaintiff's ownership extended to the centerline of the abandoned easement.

Any person who claims ownership of an abandoned railroad easement contrary to the presumption established by G.S. 1-44.2 has one year from the date of the abandonment of the easement to bring a court action to establish the claim of ownership.[44]

§ 103. Characteristics of Different Types of Owners

Introduction

Real property is owned by business firms and associations as well as by individual persons. A single parcel of land may also be owned concurrently by several persons. This section first discusses the characteristics of four types of nonindividual ownership: corporations, partnerships, limited liability companies, and unincorporated associations, and then discusses three forms of concurrent ownership: tenancy by the entireties, joint tenancy, and tenancy in common.

Corporations

Corporations are authorized to acquire, own, and convey real property.[45] Property owned by a corporation is owned by the corporation as a distinct legal entity and is not regarded as property of the shareholders.[46] Ordinarily, a corporate deed must be signed by the president, vice-president, or assistant vice-president, or similar officer. It may be attested by a secretary or assistant secretary and sealed with the corporate seal, but neither attestation nor sealing is required.[47]

Partnerships

A partnership may own real property in its own name, distinct from the individual partners.[48] A partner may convey partnership property by executing a deed to the property on behalf of the partnership.[49]

Limited Liability Companies

A limited liability company is a form of business organization that shares some characteristics of a partnership and some of a corporation; for purposes of real property transactions, it operates more like a corporation. A limited liability company is authorized to buy, sell, and hold real property in its own name.[50] Most of the deeds and other real property instruments of a limited liability company will be executed on behalf of the company by a manager or member.[51]

Unincorporated Associations

Unincorporated associations formed for charitable, fraternal, religious, social, or patriotic purposes may acquire and convey real property.[52] Conveyances must be signed by the association's chairperson or president and secretary or treasurer,[53] or by its trustee.[54]

Tenancy by the Entirety

A tenancy by the entirety is a form of concurrent ownership that can only be held by a husband and wife.[55] A tenancy by the entirety is created when property is conveyed to

1. A named man "and wife," or
2. A named woman "and husband," or

3. Two named persons, whether or not identified in the conveyance as husband and wife, if at the time of conveyance they are legally married; unless a contrary intention is expressed in the conveyance.[56]

Both spouses have an equal right to the income from and control of the entireties property, and both must join in a conveyance of the property.[57] One of the characteristics of the tenancy by the entirety is that the husband and wife, as a unit, are regarded as owning the entire property, rather than each of them owning an undivided one-half interest in the property.[58] An extension of this characteristic is that each spouse has a right of survivorship; that is, at the death of one spouse, the survivor becomes sole owner of the property as a matter of law.[59] Although at common law a tenancy by the entirety could exist only in real property, such a tenancy may be created in North Carolina in a mobile home, whether it is regarded as real or personal property.[60] When a husband and wife who own property as tenants by the entireties obtain a divorce, the tenancy by the entirety is converted into a tenancy in common, and each then owns an undivided one-half interest in the property.[61] Usually marital property will be conveyed to one spouse or the other as part of a separation agreement or divorce decree, but if it is not, then the tenancy by the entirety is converted into a tenancy in common as a matter of law.

Joint Tenancy

The joint tenancy is a rare form of concurrent ownership today. It is created when a grantor or devisor conveys land by the same instrument at the same time to two or more persons as joint tenants.[62] The joint tenancy shares the characteristic of the tenancy by the entirety that each joint tenant owns the entire property.[63] At common law the joint tenancy carried a right of survivorship, the same as the tenancy by the entirety.[64] In North Carolina, however, the automatic right of survivorship as an attribute of a joint tenancy has been abolished by statute,[65] so that at the death of a joint tenant his or her share passes by will or intestate succession just as it would for a tenant in common (discussed below). The same statute, however, provides that a right of survivorship can still be created by deed or other instrument creating the joint tenancy,[66] and occasionally mappers may see instruments in which this has been done.

Tenancy in Common

The tenancy in common is a form of concurrent ownership in which two or more persons own undivided interests in the same parcel of land, with no right of survivorship.[67] There is no requirement that each tenant in common must have acquired the interest at the same time, or by the same instrument, or even that each tenant hold the same interest; that is, one tenant may hold an undivided one-fourth interest, another tenant an undivided one-sixth interest, and so forth.[68] Each tenant is free to convey his or her interest in the property,[69] and at death, a tenant's interest is controlled by will or by the laws of intestate succession.[70] Any cotenant may request that the property be partitioned, that is, that the property be divided and each cotenant be apportioned his or her share.[71] A partitioning is a special proceeding before the clerk of superior court.[72] Partitioning the property in kind is favored over sale of the property and allotment of the proceeds to the cotenants.[73] The commissioners who oversee the partitioning are authorized to have a map made of the property showing each cotenant's boundary lines,[74] and this map will be recorded with the confirmed report of the proceedings in the register of deeds' office.[75] As a substitute for a special proceeding to partition the property, the cotenants may agree among themselves as to how it should be partitioned and may exchange deeds to effect the agreement.[76] Each deed must, of course, contain an adequate description of the cotenant's allotted part.

§ 104. How Interests in Land Are Created and Ownership Is Transferred

Introduction

Interests in land may be created and transferred in a number of different ways. The two most common methods, by will and deed, are given extended discussion at the end of this section.

Dedication of easements was discussed in Section 103, above. Here, the following methods will be discussed briefly: condemnation, judgment in a quiet title action, adverse possession, and intestate succession.

Condemnation

Agencies of state government, local governments, and private entities that exercise certain quasi-public functions, such as public utilities, have the power of eminent domain.[77] Through the exercise of this power they are authorized to take, or condemn, private land for a public use. They may condemn a fee simple estate or an easement or other interest.[78] They must pay just compensation for the land that is condemned.[79] The procedures that local governments and private condemnors must follow are set forth in Chapter 40A of the General Statutes. In condemnation actions by a private condemnor, the condemnor files a petition with the clerk of superior court,[80] which is indexed in the Index to Special Proceedings;[81] the petition is also indexed as a notice of lis pendens in the clerk's Index to Judgments, Liens, and Lis Pendens.[82] When a local government condemns land, it must file a complaint containing a declaration of taking with the clerk of superior court[83] and a memorandum of the condemnation action in the register of deeds' office.[84] A certified copy of the final judgment in the action is required to be recorded and indexed in the register of deeds' office.[85]

Although several statutes establish procedures for condemnation actions by state agencies, the ones likely to be of the most interest to property mappers are those governing actions by the Department of Transportation, and they are contained in Article 9, Chapter 136, of the General Statutes. To institute a condemnation action, the Department of Transportation files a complaint and declaration of taking with the clerk of superior court.[86] At the same time the department must file a memorandum of the action with the register of deeds.[87] The department may condemn either an easement or a fee simple estate in the property.[88] A certified copy of the final judgment in a condemnation action is required to be recorded and indexed in the register of deeds' office.[89]

Judgment in a Quiet Title Action

Any person who believes that another person has an adverse claim or interest in real property in which he or she has an estate or interest may bring an action to determine those adverse claims and quiet title to the property.[90] The judgment in the action may transfer ownership to all or a portion of the property. The judgment will be indexed in the clerk of superior court's Index to Liens, Judgments, and Lis Pendens, and a certified copy of the judgment may be registered in the register of deeds' office.[91]

Adverse Possession

Adverse possession is a means by which a claimant may acquire title to property by meeting certain statutory requirements, even though the claimant has no document of title, or has a document of title that is defective. North Carolina provides two ways that title may be acquired by adverse possession. The first is when the claimant has no document of title but adversely possesses the property for twenty years.[92] This possession must be "under known and visible lines and boundaries adversely to all other persons."[93] The elements of this possession are that the claimant must be in actual possession of the land, such possession must be hostile to the true owner and must be open and notorious, and it must be continuous and uninterrupted for the statutory period.[94] It need not, however, be intentional; the claimant may hold an honest, though mistaken, belief that the land was rightfully his or hers and still acquire title by adverse possession.[95]

The second means is possession for seven years under color of title.[96] "Color of title" means that the title document under which the claimant claims the property is somehow defective, possibly because of a formal defect in the deed or will, or because the grantor or devisor was not competent to execute the instrument or did not own the property at the time of execution.[97] The possession must be "under known and visible lines and boundaries."[98] The legislature has facilitated meeting this requirement by providing that if boundaries are marked on the ground, and a map prepared from a survey is recorded showing the boundaries, and the claimant lists the property for taxes and pays the taxes, then these acts shall constitute prima facie evidence of possession under known and visible lines and boundaries.[99]

Intestate Succession

When an owner of real property dies without a valid will, the property goes to the owner's heirs as directed by state statutes known as intestate succession statutes.[100] Title to the land passes to the heirs at the time of the owner's death.[101] The deceased person's estate is administered by an administrator who qualifies before the clerk of superior court, and preference is given to the spouse and heirs of the decedent.[102] If no qualified person comes forward to apply for letters of administration, the estate is administered by the public administrator.[103] The estate proceedings are recorded and indexed in the estate files in the clerk's office.

Wills

A will is a document by which a landowner, at death, may direct the disposition of his or her property. A will is revocable during the landowner's lifetime, and it applies only to property owned at the time of death.[104] To be valid, a will must conform to certain requirements regarding signatures and witnesses.[105] After the death of the testator (the person who made the will), the will has to be probated (proved to be genuine) by the clerk of court before the estate can be administered under the terms of the will.[106] The estate is administered by the executor, who is usually named in the will. At the time of the testator's death, title to real property vests in the heirs, that is, in the persons who would receive the property under the intestate succession statutes.[107] Once the will is probated, however, title to the property vests in the devisees (the persons named in the will to receive the property) and the vesting relates back to the time of the testator's death.[108] Many wills do not contain a legal description of the land being devised. Instead, the testator uses such general descriptions as "All my real and personal property I give to my wife Susan," or "I give my daughter Elizabeth the property known as the Smith place on Joe Moore Road in Buzzard's Creek Township." In cases such as these a property mapper must find the description in the deed or other instrument granting the property to the testator to obtain a legal description of the property. Estates administered under a will are filed and indexed in the estate records in the clerk of superior court's office.

Deeds

Elements

Interests in real property must be transferred by a written document; an oral agreement will not be enforced.[109] The document used to transfer interests in real property is the deed. The elements that a deed must contain are the names of the grantor (person conveying the interest) and grantee; a description of the land or interest in land being conveyed (property descriptions are discussed in Section 105); words of conveyance—that is, language indicating that the grantor is transferring his or her interest to the grantee; warranties, if the instrument is a warranty deed; and the grantor's signature.[110] A deed does not have to be dated.[111] To be effective in conveying the grantor's interest, the deed must be delivered to the grantee or the grantee's agent and accepted by the grantee.[112] Except for gift deeds,[113] a properly executed deed may be perfectly valid as between the parties thereto even though the instrument is never registered.[114] The purpose of registration is to protect the grantee against subsequent purchasers and creditors of the grantor.[115] Before a deed can be registered in the register of deeds' office, the execution thereof must be proved or acknowledged before a qualified official (usually a notary public),[116] and the acknowledgment or proof of execution must be certified as correct by the register of deeds.[117]

Types of Deeds

General Warranty Deed. In a general warranty deed the grantor warrants, or guarantees, the title to the property that has been transferred to the grantee. The grantor, in effect, stands behind the title and will make good to the grantee any loss incurred from a defect in or encumbrance on the title, regardless of when the defect or encumbrance occurred.[118]

Special Warranty Deed. In a special warranty deed, the grantor only warrants to make good any loss the grantee incurs as a result of a defect or encumbrance that occurred during the time the grantor held title to the property. The grantor thereby limits the time period of warranty.[119]

Quitclaim Deed. In a quitclaim deed, the grantor makes no warranties, but simply conveys whatever interest, if any, he or she has in the property.[120] If the grantor does have an interest in the property, a quitclaim deed is just as effective as a warranty deed in conveying that interest to the grantor, but one does not need to have an interest, or even think one has an interest in the property, to execute a quitclaim deed. And this can create problems for property mappers when they attempt to determine ownership for tax or other purposes. These issues are discussed in Chapter III, Listing Real Property for Taxation.

Sheriff's, Commissioner's, and Trustee's Deeds. These are deeds that convey land as a result of legal proceedings. A sheriff may execute a deed as part of an execution sale or as the result of an in rem tax foreclosure sale. A commissioner may execute a deed as part of a judicial sale or as the result of a mortgage-style tax foreclosure. A trustee may execute a deed in a proceeding to foreclose a deed of trust under a power of sale. All of these are in the nature of quitclaim deeds; they usually do not contain warranties. In each case the sheriff, commissioner, or trustee is conveying property owned by someone else, and the deed almost always recites the owner's name. The register of deeds is required to index sheriff's, commissioner's, and trustee's deeds in the names of both the sheriff, commissioner, or trustee and in the name of the owner of the property.[121]

§ 105. Property Descriptions

Introduction

For a deed to convey land it must contain a legally adequate description of the land being conveyed. This requirement of legal adequacy has been stated in the following words: "[A] deed conveying land within the meaning of the statute of frauds, G.S. 22-2, must contain a description of the land, the subject matter of the deed, either certain in itself or capable of being reduced to certainty by reference to something extrinsic to which the deed refers."[122] What this means is that the deed either must contain a description from which the land can be located on the ground—such as an accurate metes and bounds description or reference to a plat—or a description that is capable of being made certain by testimony. But testimony will not be permitted to correct, or make specific, a faulty metes and bounds description.[123] For example, the following calls in a metes and bounds description were found to be so ambiguous as to make the description legally deficient: "thence south 36 deg. east to the back line; thence with said back line to B. F. Ormond's line in Poley Ridge Branch" (the back line was not identified).[124] On the other hand, the following descriptions have been held legally adequate: "My house and lot in the town of Jefferson, N.C."; "Her house and lot north of Kinston"; and "My farm."[125] These descriptions were adequate because in each case testimony could be used to show that the grantor owned only one house and lot in the town or only one farm.

Types of Property Descriptions

Several types of descriptions are used to meet the requirement that the land being conveyed must be adequately described. The ones discussed here are those most commonly used. They are sometimes used in combination.

Metes and Bounds

A metes and bounds description is a means of describing land by using a starting point (point of beginning) and then laying off the boundaries, the perimeter, of the land described. From the description, a land surveyor should be able to locate the land and draw a map of its boundaries. A metes and bounds description typically uses a combination of monuments, courses, and distances. Monuments are fixed objects or geographical features. The following have been held to be calls to monuments: a wall,[126] the property line of another,[127] a road or highway,[128] a ditch,[129] and marked trees.[130] A call to a stake is not a call to a monument.[131]

Distances are typically stated in feet or meters, but may be stated in links (7.92 inches), rods (16 1/2 feet), or chains (66 feet).[132]

The course (direction) of a boundary line may be stated in either of two ways. It may simply be run to a monument (usually for a certain distance), as, for example, "thence 150 feet to a blazed white oak tree." More commonly, the course is stated in terms of a bearing in degrees and minutes, as, for example, "thence north 20 degrees, 15 minutes east, 150 feet to a blazed oak tree." In this example the boundary line is terminated by a monument, but a line stated in terms of bearings may be a free line, with no termination by a monument.[133] Bearings are always stated in terms of north and south,[134] depending on the direction of travel of the line. Perhaps the best way to illustrate this point is by showing how the lines would be plotted by using a protractor.[135] If a call reads "north 20 degrees, 15 minutes east, 150 feet to a blazed white oak tree," the center of the base of the protractor would be placed at the point of beginning of the call with the top of the protractor pointed due north of the point of beginning, and the line would be drawn through the 20 degree, 15 minute, mark on the east (right) side of the protractor. Due north is 00 degrees, and 20 degrees, 15 minutes, would be marked off to the right of the due north mark. If the next call is "south 10 degrees, 10 minutes west, 300 feet" (a free line), the center of the base of the protractor would be placed at the terminus of the line from the last call with the top of the protractor pointed due south of the point, and the line would be drawn through the 10 degree, 10 minute, mark on the west (left) side of the protractor. Due south is 00 degrees, and 10 degrees, 10 minutes, would be marked off to the left of the due south mark. This process is repeated until the line encloses the property.

If a call to a monument is to a street, highway, alley, or ditch, the call is to the center line, provided the grantor owned the property to the center line and there are no words in the deed to indicate a contrary intent.[136] Of course the grantor can, by appropriate language, restrict the description to the edge of the road, street, or ditch.[137]

Reference to a Map or Plat

Property may be described by reference to a map or plat, or by lot description on a plat, and the effect is to incorporate the map or plat in the deed as part of the description.[138] Usually the reference is to a recorded map or plat, as, for example, "as shown on the map of the Charles Williams property dated August 19, 1957, recorded in plat book 5, page 33, in the Chatham County registry," or "being lot 13, block II, Budden Brook subdivision, recorded in plat book 7, page 10, Orange County registry." But a deed may describe the property by reference to an unrecorded map or plat, and that is a valid description.[139]

Reference to a Prior Conveyance

A deed may refer to the description of the property as it appears in a prior conveyance. For example, it may make a reference such as "being the property described in the deed from M. B. Allen to Sloan Ford, dated March 15, 1946, and recorded in the

Davie County registry at book 190, page 24." The effect of such a reference is to incorporate the description from the earlier instrument into the present one.[140]

Quantity or Acreage

Descriptions of quantity or acreage are frequently given in deeds, but they are not regarded as boundary descriptions.[141] Instead, they provide supplementary information to the boundary description. After a metes and bounds description, one frequently finds a description of quantity in the terms, for example, "containing 150 acres, more or less."

Resolution of Inconsistent Descriptions

The description of property in an instrument occasionally contains inconsistencies or conflicts, and mappers need to know the rules by which these inconsistencies are resolved. The problem can arise in two ways: there may be inconsistencies among the calls of a metes and bounds description, or the property may be described both by metes and bounds and by a map reference, and there may be a conflict between the two.

Inconsistent Metes and Bounds Description

The object of the rules that have been developed to resolve inconsistencies is to implement the intention of the grantor and grantee.[142] To do this the courts have developed rules of precedence so that certain calls in a metes and bounds description are said to control other calls, if there is an inconsistency. The rules of precedence are as follows:

1. A call to a natural monument (marked tree or road, for example) controls a call to an artificial monument (property line of another, for example).[143]
2. Monuments control courses.[144]
3. Courses control distances.[145]
4. Recitals of quantity are the least reliable description.[146]

The application of these rules can be illustrated by the following examples. Suppose the call is "north 12 degrees, 10 minutes east, 200 feet to a concrete marker," but the marker is 190 feet from the point of beginning. The line should be run 190 feet; the call to the monument controls the distance call. Suppose the call is "south 00 degrees, 09 minutes west, 100 feet to a stake," but the stake is actually on a bearing of south 00 degrees, 45 minutes west, 90 feet. The line should follow the course and distance in the call; a stake is not a monument. Suppose at the end of a metes and bounds description a quantity of 120 acres, more or less, is recited, but that when the boundaries are plotted on the basis of the metes and bounds description and the quantity is computed, the quantity is 100 acres. The metes and bounds description controls.

Conflict between Description and Reference to Map

When an instrument describes property both by metes and bounds and by reference to a block and lot shown on a map or plat, and there is a conflict between the two, the reference to the map or plat is the controlling description.[147]

Water Boundaries

Special rules apply when the boundary or reference point in a description is a river, stream, sound, or the Atlantic Ocean. If the boundary stream or river is non-navigable, a call that runs with the line of the stream, or along the stream, is a call to the midpoint of the stream.[148] If the boundary is a navigable river or lake, the line runs with the bank. This is so because title to the bed and banks of navigable waters is in the state,[149] and the state is forbidden to convey a fee interest in such lands.[150] A call to the high water mark of a non-navigable sound has been held to carry the line to the high water mark.[151] A call for a boundary line that runs to or with the Atlantic Ocean carries the line to the mean high tide line;[152] the state owns the foreshore and seaward three geographical miles.[153]

Notes

1. Ingold v. Phoenix Assurance Co., Ltd., 230 N.C. 142, 52 S.E.2d 366 (1949).
2. Hoilman v. Johnson, 164 N.C. 268, 80 S.E. 249 (1913).
3. Chandler v. Cameron, 229 N.C. 62, 47 S.E.2d 528 (1948).
4. Flynt v. Conrad, 61 N.C. 190 (1867).
5. N.C. GEN. STAT. § 105-273(13).
6. J. WEBSTER, JR., WEBSTER'S REAL ESTATE LAW IN NORTH CAROLINA § 2-1 (P. Hetrick & J. McLaughlin, Jr., eds. 5th ed. 1999).

7. *See* Lee-Moore Oil Co. v. Cleary, 295 N.C. 417, 245 S.E.2d 720 (1978), and WEBSTER, *supra* note 6, §§ 2-2, 2-3, and 2-4.

8. WEBSTER, *supra* note 6, § 3-1.

9. C. MOYNIHAN, INTRODUCTION TO THE LAW OF REAL PROPERTY 28 (1962).

10. *See* WEBSTER, *supra* note 6, §6-1.

11. *See* Moche v. Leno, 227 N.C. 159, 41 S.E.2d 369 (1947).

12. *See* ch. 42, N.C. GEN. STAT.

13. *See* William v. Sealy, 201 N.C. 372, 160 S.E. 452 (1931), and WEBSTER, *supra* note 6, § 4-1.

14. N.C. GEN. STAT. § 39-7.

15. *Id.* § 29-30.

16. *See* Price v. Bunn, 13 N.C. App. 652, 187 S.E.2d 423 (1972), and MOYNIHAN, *supra* note 9, at 35–36.

17. Brittain v. Taylor, 168 N.C. 271, 84 S.E. 280 (1915), and MOYNIHAN, *supra* note 9, at 36–37.

18. N.C. Gen. Stat. § 41-32.

19. MOYNIHAN, *supra* note 9, at 48, and *see, e.g.,* Tillet v. Nixon, 180 N.C. 195, 104 S.E. 352 (1920).

20. MOYNIHAN, *supra* note 9, at 94.

21. *Id.* at 110.

22. WEBSTER, *supra* note 6, § 5-7, and *see* Roe v. Journigan, 181 N.C. 180, 106 S.E. 680 (1921).

23. Davis v. Robinson, 189 N.C. 589, 127 S.E. 697 (1925).

24. WEBSTER, *supra* note 6, § 15-2.

25. Shingleton v. State, 260 N.C. 451, 133 S.E.2d 183 (1963).

26. *Id.*

27. *Id.*

28. WEBSTER, *supra* note 6, § 15-4.

29. *Id.* § 15-6.

30. *Id.* § 15-7.

31. Sections 121-34 through 121-42 of the N.C. General Statutes provide for such easements in the form of "conservation agreements." These statutes remove the disabilities that would otherwise impair the enforcement of a conservation easement in gross. See especially N.C. GEN. STAT. § 121-38.

32. Webster discusses ten ways of creating an easement. *See* WEBSTER, *supra* note 6, §§ 5-8 through 15-21.

33. *Id.* § 15-9.

34. *Id.* § 15-10.

35. *Id.* § 15-17.

36. D. LAWRENCE, PROPERTY INTERESTS IN NORTH CAROLINA STREETS 4 (Institute of Government, The University of North Carolina at Chapel Hill 1985).

37. *Id.* at 5–7.

38. *Id.* at 5.

39. *Id.* at 16.

40. *Id.*

41. *See* BLACK'S LAW DICTIONARY 1326 (7th ed. 1999).

42. McLaurin v. Winston-Salem Southbound Ry., 323 N.C. 609, 374 S.E.2d 265 (1988).

43. 335 N.C. 133, 436 S.E.2d 122 (1993).

44. N.C. GEN. STAT. § 1-44.2(b).

45. *Id.* § 55-3-02(4) & (5), and, for nonprofit corporations, § 55A-15(b)(1) & (2).

46. Marshall v. Western N.C. R.R. Co., 92 N.C. 322 (1885).

47. *See* N.C. GEN. STAT. § 47-41.01.

48. *Id.* § 59-38.

49. *Id.* § 59-40.

50. *Id.* § 57C-2-02(3) & (4).

51. *See id.* § 57C-3-25(c).

52. *Id.* § 39-24.

53. *Id.* § 39-25.

54. *Id.* § 39-26.

55. WEBSTER, *supra* note 6, § 7-4.

56. N.C. GEN. STAT. § 39-13.6.

57. *Id.*

58. MOYNIHAN, *supra* note 9, at 229.

59. Davis v. Bass, 188 N.C. 200, 124 S.E. 566 (1924).

60. N.C. GEN. STAT. § 41-2.5.

61. Lanier v. Dawes, 255 N.C. 458, 121 S.E.2d 857 (1961).

62. WEBSTER, *supra* note 6, § 7-2.

63. *Id.*

64. *Id.*

65. N.C. GEN. STAT. § 41-2.

66. *Id.*

67. WEBSTER, *supra* note 6, § 7-3.

68. *Id.*

69. *Id.* § 7-6.

70. *Id.* § 7-5.

71. N.C. GEN. STAT. § 46-3.

72. *Id.* § 46-1.

73. *Id.* § 46-22.

74. *Id.* § 46-18.

75. *Id.* § 46-20.

76. *See* Smith v. Smith, 249 N.C. 669, 107 S.E.2d 530 (1959).

77. WEBSTER, *supra* note 6, § 19-1.

78. *See* N.C. GEN. STAT. § 40A-2.

79. WEBSTER, *supra* note 6, § 19-1.

80. N.C. GEN. STAT. § 40A-20.

81. *See id.* § 40A-19.

82. *Id.* § 40A-21.

83. *Id.* § 40A-41. This is a civil action rather than a special proceeding.

84. *Id.* § 40A-43.

85. *Id.* § 40A-54.

86. *Id.* § 136-103. This is also a civil action.

87. *Id.* § 136-104.

88. *See id.* § 136-103.

89. *Id.* § 136-116.

90. *Id.* § 41-10.

91. *Id.* § 1-228.

92. *Id.* § 1-40.

93. *Id.*

94. WEBSTER, *supra* note 6, § 14-3.

95. Walls v. Grohman, 315 N.C. 239, 337 S.E.2d 556 (1985). This case overruled a line of decisions holding to the contrary.

96. N.C. GEN. STAT. § 1-38.

97. WEBSTER, *supra* note 6, § 14-11.

98. N.C. GEN. STAT. § 1-38.

99. *Id.*

100. *See* ch. 29 N.C. GEN. STAT., especially §§ 29-14, 29-15, & 29-16.

101. N.C. GEN. STAT. § 28A-15-2(b).

102. *Id.* §§ 28A-4-1(b) & 28A-6-1.

103. *Id.* § 28A-12-4.

104. T. ATKINSON, HANDBOOK OF THE LAW OF WILLS 1 (2d ed. 1953).

105. *See* N.C. GEN. STAT. §§ 31-3.3, 31-3.4, & 31-11.6.

106. *Id.* §§ 31-18.1, 28A-4-1, & 28A-13-1.

107. *Id.* § 28A-15-2(b).

108. *Id.* §§ 28A-15-2(b) & 31-39.

109. *Id.* § 22-2.

110. WEBSTER, *supra* note 6, § 10-6.

111. *See* New Hope Building Supply Co. v. Nations, 259 N.C. 681, 131 S.E.2d 425 (1963).

112. WEBSTER, *supra* note 6, § 10-5.

113. Like other deeds, a deed of gift is not effective as to creditors or purchasers for value from the grantor until it is registered. Unlike other deeds, however, it becomes void even as between the parties if it is not registered within two years after the date of its execution. N.C. GEN. STAT. § 47-26.

114. *See, e.g.,* Patterson v. Bryant, 216 N.C. 550, 5 S.E.2d 849 (1939).

115. *See* N.C. GEN. STAT. § 47-18.

116. *Id.* § 47-17.

117. *Id.* § 47-14.

118. WEBSTER, *supra* note 6, § 10-3.

119. *Id.*

120. *Id.* § 10-4.

121. N.C. GEN. STAT. § 161-22.1.

122. Powell v. Mills, 237 N.C. 582, 588, 75 S.E.2d 759, 765 (1953).

123. *Id.*

124. *Id.* at 589, 75 S.E.2d at 765.

125. North Carolina Self Help Corp. v. Brinkley, 215 N.C. 615, 2 S.E.2d 889 (1939).

126. Cutts v. Casey, 271 N.C. 165, 155 S.E.2d 519 (1967).

127. Batson v. Bell, 249 N.C. 718, 107 S.E.2d 562 (1959).

128. Franklin v. Faulkner, 248 N.C. 656, 104 S.E.2d 841 (1958).

129. *Id.*

130. Green v. Barker, 254 N.C. 603, 119 S.E.2d 456 (1961).

131. Tice v. Winchester, 225 N.C. 673, 36 S.E.2d 257 (1954).

132. C. BROWN, BOUNDARY CONTROL AND LEGAL PRINCIPLES 8 (2d ed. 1969).

133. *Id.* at 17.

134. *Id.*

135. *See* 1 C. FLICK, ABSTRACT AND TITLE PRACTICE § 254 (2d ed. 1958).

136. WEBSTER, *supra* note 6, § 10-39.

137. *Id.*

138. Kelly v. King, 225 N.C. 709, 36 S.E.2d 220 (1945).

139. North Carolina Highway Comm'n v. Wortman, 4 N.C. App. 546, 167 S.E.2d 462 (1969).

140. Williams v. Bailey, 178 N.C. 630, 101 S.E. 105 (1919).

141. WEBSTER, *supra* note 6, § 10-43.

142. *Id.* § 10-37.

143. BROWN, *supra* note 131, at 134.

144. Cutts v. Casey, 271 N.C. 165, 155 S.E.2d 519 (1967).

145. Tice v. Winchester, 225 N.C. 673, 36 S.E.2d 257 (1954).

146. *Id.*

147. Kelly v. King, 225 N.C. 709, 36 S.E.2d 220 (1945), and Nash v. Wilmington & Weldon R.R. Co., 67 N.C. 413 (1872).

148. Rose v. Franklin, 216 N.C. 289, 4 S.E.2d 876 (1939).

149. N.C. GEN. STAT. § 146-64(6) and (7), and *see* Swan Island Club, Inc. v. White, 114 F. Supp. 95 (E.D.N.C. 1953), *aff'd*, 209 F.2d 698 (4th Cir. 1954), and Murray v. Sermon, 8 N.C. 56 (1820).

150. N.C. GEN. STAT. § 146-3.

151. Kelly v. King, 225 N.C. 709, 36 S.E.2d 220 (1945).

152. Carolina Beach Fishing Pier, Inc. v. Town of Carolina Beach, 277 N.C. 297, 177 S.E.2d 513 (1970).

153. N.C. GEN. STAT. § 146-64, and West v. Slick, 313 N.C. 33, 326 S.E.2d 601 (1985).

II. Property Records and Establishing the Chain of Title

§ 200. Introduction

This chapter has two purposes. The first is to acquaint the property mapper with the land records kept in four offices: the register of deeds, the clerk of superior court, the municipal clerk, and the clerk to the board of county commissioners. In addition to identifying the types of records, the chapter discusses the indexing systems for the records. The second purpose is to introduce the mapper to techniques for establishing the chain of title to a particular parcel of real property. After a general discussion about establishing the chain of title, two examples are given to illustrate how the chain would be built in particular instances.

The types of indexes and indexing practices, as well as record-keeping practices, in the clerk of superior court's offices are standardized across the state by statute and by rules promulgated by the Administrative Office of the Courts.[1] Examiners of these indexes and records should find few local variations among the several counties. Since January 1, 1995, the registers of deeds have been required to index all real property instruments according to minimum indexing standards prepared by the secretary of state.[2] Each register's office has several copies of these standards, and frequent users of the records should familiarize themselves with them. Indexes in use before 1995 may show considerable local variations in how different types of names are indexed. No similar state agency requires uniformity of indexing practices in the other two offices discussed in this chapter, the municipal clerk and the clerk to the board of county commissioners.

§ 201. Records in the Office of the Register of Deeds

Deeds, Deeds of Trust, Leases, Option Agreements, and Easements

Deeds, deeds of trust, leases, option agreements, and ease-ments account for most of the land records in the register of deeds' office. In some offices the recording medium is still paper and the records are bound in books. Some offices maintain the records on microfilm, and in these offices the typical arrange-ment is to place the film in reels where it can be viewed in reader-printers and a copy of the document can be made, if de-sired. Many offices scan the documents to an optical disk, CD, or other electronic medium. These records can then be viewed by means of a personal computer, and some counties are providing Internet access to the records.

Deeds, deeds of trust, leases, option agreements, and ease-ments are accessible through the grantor-grantee indexes. In the grantor index the name of the grantor, or grantors, of each in-strument is entered alphabetically, with a reference to the book and page number where the instrument is recorded. Other infor-mation that is typically shown on the index line is the date the instrument was recorded, the names of the grantees, the type of instrument (usually abbreviated), and a brief description of the property affected by the instrument. In the grantee index the name of the grantee, or grantees, of each instrument is set out in alphabetical order, usually followed on the index line by the names of the grantors and the same information that is entered on the grantor index.

The secretary of state's indexing standards require that the names be indexed in straight alphabetical order, whether on the grantor index or on the grantee index. To comply with this re-quirement, virtually all registers of deeds have computerized their indexes. In many offices, this allows both the index search to be made from a personal computer and the document itself, once located, to be viewed and copied from the same computer.

Two counties, Orange and Chowan, maintain indexes by the parcel identifier number (PIN) of the land involved. In these counties, once the PIN is ascertained, either by an examination of the property maps or other means, all of the index entries for instruments affecting that parcel can be called up by entering the PIN in the computer.

Corporations, Partnerships, and Assumed Names

In most registers' offices, records of corporations, partnerships, and assumed names are in books separate from the land records, although statutory authority exists for recording them in the same books with the land records.[3] The indexing standards require that the index entries for corporations, partnerships, and assumed names be included in the consolidated real property index, although older records may have one index for corporations and another for partnerships and assumed names. In the record of corporations the searcher can find a copy of the corporate charter, which will list the names of the incorporators, and any amendments to the charter. In the partnership records the searcher can find the names of the partners who make up the partnership, and in the assumed name records, the searcher can find the name of the individual, partnership, or corporation that is doing business under an assumed name. Since July 1, 1990, corporate charters and related documents have been recorded in the office of the secretary of state only; copies are not recorded with the local register of deeds.[4]

Maps and Plats

The traditional method of recording maps and plats in the register's office was to place them in large plat books, and this is the method still used in some counties. Most counties today, however, either record maps and plats on microfilm or place the maps and plats in hanging files in map cabinets. Maps and plats are indexed in the consolidated real property index. They are indexed alphabetically by the name of the landowner and, if a subdivision plat is involved, by the name of the subdivision, with a reference to the plat book, film card, or cabinet where the record copy can be found. Registers of deeds are required to retain either the original map or plat presented for recording or a master copy of it,[5] and these are usually filed in map drawers. Property mappers may occasionally need to see the original map to determine its scale or to verify some detail that does not clearly appear on the record copy.

Condominium plans are filed either in the plat books or in a special set of condominium books.[6] They should be indexed by the name of the owner and by the name of the condominium.

UCC Financing Statements

Mappers may occasionally need to examine Uniform Commercial Code (UCC) financing statements, especially those that create a security interest in fixtures (generally known as "fixture filings"). The register of deeds gives each recorded financing statement a number and then places it in a special envelope, or shuck, and places the envelope in numerical order in a file drawer. UCC financing statements are indexed in the Debtor Index to Financing Statements alphabetically by name of the debtor. The index entry, in addition to showing the name of the debtor in the statement, shows the filing number of the statement (thus indicating where it can be located), the filing date, and the name of the secured party. Fixture filings must also be indexed in the real property grantor-grantee indexes. In the real property indexes the debtor is indexed as the grantor and the secured party as the grantee.

After July 1, 2001, the only financing statements filed in the register of deeds office will be real-property related statements such as fixture filings. These will be indexed in the real property index and recorded in the real property records.

§ 202. Records in the Office of the Clerk of Superior Court

Introduction

Records in the clerk of superior court's office are usually kept in case files (summaries of which are placed in docket books) while the case is active and then are microfilmed, so the records themselves are not accessible in books as they are in the register of deeds' office. Each clerk's office contains four indexes relating to civil matters, and these indexes are uniform in all counties. The types of records contained in each index are discussed below.

Index to Civil Actions

Every civil action filed is indexed in the Index to Civil Actions. The indexing is alphabetical by the name of the defendant in the action, and the index entry also gives the date the action was filed, the file number, and the name of the plaintiff. Condemnation actions by local governments[7] and by the Department of Transportation,[8] quiet title actions,[9] and divorce actions[10] are indexed here. This index is computerized in all 100 counties.

Index to Special Proceedings

Civil matters filed in the clerk's office that are not civil actions or estate proceedings are special proceedings and are indexed in the Index to Special Proceedings by the name of the person who filed the special proceeding and cross-indexed by the name of any other party to the proceeding. Deed of trust foreclosures under a power of sale,[11] condemnation actions by private condemnors,[12] partition proceedings,[13] proceedings to establish property boundaries,[14] and name changes[15] are indexed in this index. The index entry gives the date the proceeding was filed, a brief description of the proceeding, and the file and docket number where the papers relevant to the proceeding may be located. This index is computerized in some counties.

Index to Judgments, Liens, and Lis Pendens

Judgments that are docketed, liens—such as state and federal tax liens, and notices of lis pendens—are indexed in the Index to Judgments, Liens, and Lis Pendens alphabetically by the name of the defendant or person against whom the lien or notice was filed. A notice of lis pendens is a notice that a legal action has been filed and that it may affect title to real property.[16] The final judgment in a quiet title action or in a divorce action, if the judgment affected title to real property, should be indexed in this index. The index entry shows the name of the person in whose favor the judgment or lien was entered, the date of the judgment or lien, and the book and page number of the judgment docket where the instrument is abstracted. This index is computerized in all 100 counties.

Index to Estates

Proceedings involving decedents' estates are indexed in the Index to Estates under the name of the decedent. For estate proceedings involving wills, there is also an Index to Devisees, which is in the name of each devisee listed in the will. These index entries refer to the estate file number where the will and other papers are located. This index is computerized in some counties.

§ 203. Records in the Office of the Municipal Clerk

From time to time a property mapper may need to examine records in the municipal clerk's office. These records include maps or verbal descriptions of municipal boundaries, including changes made by annexations;[17] municipal ordinances, including subdivision ordinances;[18] maps of zoning districts;[19] and assessment rolls for special assessments.[20]

§ 204. Records in the Office of the Clerk to the Board of Commissioners

A property mapper may also need to consult records in the office of the clerk to the board of county commissioners. These records include maps or verbal descriptions of townships[21] and electoral districts;[22] county ordinances, including subdivision ordinances;[23] zoning maps;[24] and assessment rolls for special assessments.[25]

§ 205. Establishing the Chain of Title

Introduction

There will be times when a property mapper must trace ownership of a parcel of land backward in time. To do this, the mapper must build, or "run," the chain of title. This procedure requires the mapper to begin with the present owner of the land and work back—owner by owner—until the mapper has developed the information desired or extended the chain of title back a certain number of years. The procedure requires the use of indexes and records in both the clerk of superior court's office and the register of deeds' office. The starting point for the search, however, should be either the land records office or the county assessor's office. In one of these offices the mapper should find the current property record card (or its computerized equivalent) for the property, which should show the name of the current owner and the deed book and page or estate file where the owner's instrument of title is recorded. With this information, plus a current description of the property, the mapper is ready to begin using the indexes and records to trace the chain of title. The principal method of doing this is by finding the current owner's name in the grantee index, identifying his or her grantor, and then finding that grantor's name in the grantee index and identifying *his or her* grantor, and so on. When the searcher draws a blank, the first option should be to check the grantor's name in the Index to Devisees in the clerk's office to see if the grantor acquired the property by will, and then return to the grantee indexes in the register of deeds' office. As every experienced searcher knows, there are many complications and permutations on this basic method. Below are two examples of transfers of ownership over a number of years, bringing the story down to the current owners. After each narrative there is a step-by-step description of how a searcher would build the chain of title in this particular case.

Examples

1. On June 3, 1936, Wesley and Martha Harris sold 10 acres of their 200-acre farm to Wesley's nephew, Sidney Jackson. Sidney died on April 15, 1947, and devised the property to his daughter and son-in-law, Anne and David Morgan. On March 30, 1955, the Morgans sold 5 of the 10 acres to the Rabbit Corporation for construction of a fast-food restaurant specializing in rabbit fried in twenty-three herbs and spices and turnip-flavored biscuits. The Rabbit Corporation filed a petition in bankruptcy on February 5, 1956, and the property was sold as part of the bankruptcy liquidation to John Ralph Williams. On March 10, 1968, Waverly

County sold the property at a tax lien foreclosure sale to James and Mary Greenwood, the current owners. You are interested in the parcel owned by the Greenwoods.

    a. Check the Greenwoods in the grantee index. The deed in the tax foreclosure sale was executed by either a commissioner or the sheriff, and the entry on the index line should state that it was a commissioner's or sheriff's deed. Also, Williams, the immediately prior owner, should be listed as grantor. To be certain about what has happened, the searcher should examine the deed itself; Williams's name should be recited in the deed.

    b. Check Williams in the grantee index. The deed in the bankruptcy sale was a trustee's deed, and the Rabbit Corporation should be listed on the index as grantor. Again, to be certain about this, the searcher should examine the deed.

    c. Check the Rabbit Corporation in the grantee index. Looking under the Rs, the searcher may not find Rabbit Corporation. This is a tip-off that corporations are set out in a special part of the index; go to that part. Determine that Rabbit's grantors were Anne and David Morgan.

    d. Check the Morgans in the grantee index and draw a blank. Guess that they received the property by will or intestate succession and go to the estate records in the clerk of superior court's office. Because they had to acquire the property before 1967, look for the Devisee Index that was in effect during the period when they probably acquired the property. Under "Morgan" find that the property was devised to them by Sidney Jackson.

    e. Check Sidney Jackson in the grantee index and determine that his grantors were Wesley and Martha Harris. You have established the chain of title to the property to 1936.

    2. On September 6, 1967, Marvin and Wilma Rogers sold their 200-acre farm to Ridgewood Development Company. Ridgewood financed the purchase with a deed of trust on the property to secure a note to Big Rock Insurance Company. In 1970 Big Rock foreclosed the deed of trust and the entire tract was purchased at the foreclosure sale by Pleasant Acres, Inc. In 1972 Pleasant Acres filed a subdivision plat subdividing the tract into one-half-acre lots (Pleasant Acres Subdivision). On May 10,

1983, the city of Lone Pine, in which the property is located, condemned three of the lots for a city park. The park was never built, and in 1985, Stewart Fraser, whose house is on an adjoining lot, purchased one of the lots from the city. In 1986 Fraser sold the vacant lot to Gordon and Jane Fleetwood.

a. Check the Fleetwoods in the grantee index and determine that their grantor was Stewart Fraser.
b. Check Stewart Fraser in the grantee index and determine that his grantor was the city of Lone Pine.
c. Check the city of Lone Pine in the grantee index. This search will not show a deed to the city, but it should show the recording of a memorandum of action in a condemnation action by the city of Lone Pine (grantee) against Pleasant Acres, Inc. (grantor), to condemn certain lots. The searcher must make an educated guess that this is how the city acquired the property. From the information contained in the memorandum of action, the searcher can verify the guess by examining the file of the condemnation action in the clerk's office.
d. Check Pleasant Acres, Inc., in the grantee index to find the trustee's deed. Ridgewood Development Company should be named as grantor (the real party in interest), but the searcher should examine the deed to be sure he or she knows what happened.
e. Check Ridgewood Development Company in the grantee index and determine that its grantors were Marvin and Wilma Rogers.

Notes

1. N.C. GEN. STAT. § 7A-109.
2. *Id.* §§ 147-54.3(b) & (b1) & 161-22.3.
3. N.C. GEN. STAT. § 161-14.01.
4. *Id.* § 55-1-25, and 1989 N.C. Sess. Laws ch. 265.
5. N.C. GEN STAT. § 47-30(b).
6. *See id.* § 47C-2-109(a) and the North Carolina Comment that accompanies it.
7. *Id.* § 40A-41.
8. *Id.* § 136-103.
9. *Id.* § 41-10.

10. *Id.* § 50-8.
11. *See id.* § 45-21.16(g).
12. *Id.* § 40A-19.
13. *Id.* § 46-1.
14. *Id.* § 38-1.
15. *Id.* § 101-2.
16. *Id.* § 1-116.
17. *Id.* § 160A-22.
18. *Id.* § 160A-78.
19. *Id.* § 160A-77.
20. *Id.* §§ 160A-227 & 160A-228.
21. *Id.* § 153A-19.
22. *Id.* § 153A-20.
23. *Id.* § 153A-48.
24. *Id.* § 153A-49.
25. *Id.* §§ 153A-194 & 153A-195.

III. Listing Real Property for Taxation

§ 300. Introduction

In some counties property mappers work in the tax department, in others they work in an independent land records or mapping department. Regardless of the organizational structure in which they work, all property mappers need to understand the legal principles that govern the listing of real property for ad valorem taxes. Historically, mapping was performed as an aid in the listing and assessing process, and mapping programs were justified on the grounds that property could be more accurately listed and assessed and property that may have escaped taxation would be found. County maps serve many other governmental functions today, including land-use planning, environmental management, recording and indexing of land records, and planning for fire protection and emergency management. But a central purpose of mapping remains that of aiding the county assessor in listing and appraising property for taxes.

§ 301. Time of Listing

Significance of January 1

Under the North Carolina Machinery Act[1] January 1 is a date of critical importance. The ownership, value, and exempt status of real property are determined as of January 1 each year.[2] With one exception, it makes no difference what happens to property after

January 1: It can be sold to a new owner, even a tax-exempt organization, or improvements may be built or destroyed; the property is still taxable in the name of the owner as of January 1 and the tax value is unchanged by any events occurring after January 1.[3] The exception is that when property that was owned by an exempt owner on January 1 is sold or transferred to a nonexempt owner before July 1, the property is fully taxable for the year.[4]

The Regular Listing Period

The usual period during which property must be listed each year is the month of January.[5] In a nonrevaluation year, the board of county commissioners may extend this period for thirty days, and in a revaluation year the board may extend it for sixty days beyond the end of January. In addition to these general extensions of the listing period, the board of county commissioners may, upon written request, grant extensions to individual taxpayers; however, such extensions must not run later than April 15.[6] The board may delegate the authority to make individual extensions to the assessor.

Permanent Listing Systems

Almost all counties have in place a permanent system for listing real property for taxes, and by 2004 all counties must have adopted such a system.[7] Under a permanent listing system, the assessor assumes responsibility for listing all real property in the name of the record owner as of January 1, and the owner is relieved of the legal duty to list it.[8] The owner's responsibility is limited to reporting any new or changed improvements to the property and any separate rights in the property since the last listing date.[9] If the owner fails to report improvements, the assessor may discover the improvements under G.S. 105-312, and the late-listing penalty is limited to 10 percent of the tax on the improvements.[10] Under a permanent listing system, a discovery can still be made of the land itself, but no late-listing penalties may be imposed in such a case.

§ 302. Name of Listing Owner

Owner of Record

Several statutes deal with the name of the person or persons to whom real property must be listed each year. G.S. 105-303(b)(1) provides that in counties with permanent listing, the assessor is responsible for listing all real property in the name of the record owner as of January 1. G.S. 105-303(a) gives the assessor the means of obtaining the identity of the record owner from the register of deeds, and G.S. 105-302(c) tells the assessor who the record owner is in different kinds of real property ownership.

G.S. 105-303(a) provides two alternative procedures that a county may use to obtain the names of the record owners of property, and regardless of whether a county has installed a permanent listing system, it should adopt one of the procedures. Under the first procedure, the board of commissioners may require the register of deeds to send the assessor the following information regarding every deed or other instrument of conveyance that is recorded:

1. the name of the person conveying the property,
2. the name and address of the person to whom the property is conveyed,
3. a description of the property sufficient to locate and identify it, and
4. a statement as to whether the parcel is conveyed in whole or in part.

The register of deeds can usually fulfill this requirement by making a copy of the deed and sending it to the assessor.

Under the second procedure, the board of commissioners may require every deed and other instrument of conveyance to be presented to the assessor so that the necessary information can be obtained before the instrument can be recorded in the register of deeds' office.

A few counties use both procedures. They require the instrument to be presented to the assessor or land records manager so that information can be obtained or a PIN number assigned before recording. They then require a copy to be forwarded to the tax or land records office after recording so the book and page number where the instrument is recorded can be entered in the tax records.

In most cases, determining the name of the record owner is simply a matter of examining the relevant deed, will, or other title document. In some cases, however, questions may arise concerning who is the owner for listing purposes. Typically, these questions arise in cases of marriage, divorce, or death. It should be remembered that the listing must be in the name of the owner of record as of January 1 of the tax year in question; the assessor is never justified in making a change in the name of the listing owner merely upon the request of someone with an interest in the property. The following examples illustrate some of the most common questions that arise.

1. Jack Greene, a bachelor, owns property in his own name. He marries Judy. He asks the assessor to change the listing for the property from Jack Greene to Jack and Judy Greene. Should the change be made? No. If Jack wants this change made, he should execute a deed to Judy and himself and record it.

2. Harry and Jane Smith own property as tenants by the entirety. In September they separate and sign a separation agreement. The agreement provides that when the divorce decree is entered, Harry will execute a deed to the property to Jane. In January, before the divorce decree is entered, Harry requests that the property be listed in Jane's name alone. Should the change be made? No. The signing of the separation agreement does not change the ownership of the property; Harry and Jane still own it as tenants by the entirety. The change should be made after Harry executes the deed to Jane and the deed is recorded.

3. Shirley and Bill Hill own a parcel of real property as tenants by the entirety. Bill dies and his will is probated. Shirley asks that the property be listed in her name. Should the change be made? Yes. All that is necessary to make the change in this case is that the assessor see the deed and Bill's death certificate. The will does not govern disposition of this property.

Name of the Listing Owner—Statutory Directions

G.S. 105-302(c) contains specific directions concerning in whose name property is to be listed. Below, each subsection is quoted and commentary then follows.

(1) The owner of the equity of redemption in real property subject to a mortgage or deed of trust shall be considered the owner of the property, and such real property shall be listed in the name of the owner of the equity of redemption.

When real property is subject to a deed of trust, legal title is in the trustee. The grantor of the deed of trust (the person who owned the property and is using it as security for a loan) holds an equitable interest in the property. This subsection directs that the property be listed in the name of this equity holder—the person who has "the equity of redemption."

(2) Real property owned by a corporation shall be listed in the name of the corporation.

This listing direction simply means that corporate property is to be listed in the name of the corporation, rather than in the names of the officers or shareholders. The listing should be in the name of the corporation as set forth in the articles of incorporation, even though the corporation has filed a certificate of assumed name in the register of deeds' office pursuant to G.S. 66-68 and is doing business under that name.

(3) Real property owned by an unincorporated association shall be listed in the name of the association.

As with corporations, this provision requires that property owned by an unincorporated association be listed in the name of the association, rather than in the names of the members of the association.

(4) Real property owned by a partnership shall be listed in the name of the partnership.

Real property owned by a partnership is not to be listed in the name of each partner.

(5) Real property held in connection with a sole proprietorship shall be listed in the name of the owner, and the

name and address of the proprietorship shall be noted on the abstract.

This listing direction is applicable when an individual, not a corporation, is doing business either in his or her own name or in a trade name. Regardless of the name of the business, the property is to be listed in the name of the individual owner, and the business address is to be entered on the abstract.

> (6) Real property of which a decedent died possessed, if not under the control of an executor or administrator, shall be listed in the names of the heirs or devisees if known, but such property may be listed as property of "the heirs" or "the devisees" of the decedent, without naming them, until they have given the assessor notice of their names and of the division of the estate. It shall be the duty of an executor or administrator having control of real property to list it in his fiduciary capacity, as required by subdivision (c)(7), below, until he is divested of control of the property. However, the right of an administrator or executor of a deceased person to petition for the sale of real property to make assets shall not be considered control of the real property for the purposes of this subdivision.

This provision states the general rule that unless the property is under the control of an executor or administrator on January 1, it is to be listed in the names of the heirs or devisees[11] of the deceased owner. Although an executor or administrator may take control of the property during administration of the estate,[12] it is fairly unusual for this to happen, and before taking control the executor or administrator must petition the clerk of superior court and receive an order authorizing such control.[13] An executor or administrator with control of real property must list it under the provisions of G.S. 105-302(c)(7).

An assessor who knows the names of the heirs or devisees should list the property in their names, for example: "Faye Brown, Gloria Brown, Joseph Brown, Raymond Brown devisees." If the assessor does not know their names, then the statute authorizes the following form of listing: "Raymond Brown devisees (or heirs)." Mappers and assessors should strive to list the property in the specific names of the heirs or devisees as soon as possible. One means of facilitating this is an arrangement with the clerk of superior court whereby the clerk sends the assessor a notice of each will probated or estate administered. The mapper or assessor can then periodically check on the estate's progress, and make the proper listing as soon as the property is distributed and the estate closed.

In connection with this statute, mappers should be aware that title to real property vests in the decedent's heirs at the instant of death, but if a valid will is probated, title vests in the devisees, and the vesting relates back to the date of death.[14]

> (7) Real property, the title to which is held by a trustee, guardian, or other fiduciary, shall be listed by the fiduciary in his fiduciary capacity except as otherwise provided in this section.

When property is held by a trustee or other fiduciary, it is controlled or managed by that fiduciary for the benefit of another person, frequently the person who is the owner of record. Examples include a trustee who manages property for the benefit of minor children under the terms of trust provisions in a will, or a guardian who manages property for an incompetent person. This subsection requires the fiduciary to list the property in his or her name and to indicate the fiduciary capacity on the abstract.

> (8) A life tenant or tenant for the life of another shall be considered the owner of real property, and it shall be his duty to list the property for taxation, indicating on the abstract that he is a life tenant or tenant for the life of another named individual.

When a life tenancy or tenancy for the life of another[15] is created in real property, there are always at least two persons with interests in the property: the life tenant or tenant for the life of another, and the reversioner or remainderman. This subsection requires the life tenant or tenant for the life of another to list the property in his or her name and indicate that status on the abstract.

(9) Upon request to and with the approval of the assessor, undivided interests in real property owned by tenants in common who are not copartners may be listed by the respective owners in accordance with their respective undivided interests. Otherwise, real property held by tenants in common shall be listed in the names of all the owners.

This subsection states the general rule that property owned by tenants in common is to be listed in all of the names on a single abstract. For example, if three sisters, Betty, Alice, and Ann Smith, own a parcel of property as tenants in common, with each owning an undivided one-third interest in the property, the property would be listed on one abstract in the names of Betty, Alice, and Ann Smith. In exceptional cases, if the owners request separate listings and the assessor agrees, each owner's interest can be listed separately. For example, if the Smith sisters made such a request and the assessor allowed it, three abstracts would be prepared, each signed by Betty, Alice, or Ann, and showing that sister's one-third interest in the property.

(10) Real property owned by husband and wife as tenants by the entirety shall be listed on a single abstract in the names of both tenants, and the nature of their ownership shall be indicated thereon.

Property owned by husband and wife as tenants by the entirety is regarded as owned by the husband and wife as a unit.[16] This subsection requires the property to be listed in both names on a single abstract. Mappers should not be misled by an abstract signed by the husband alone into assuming that he is the sole owner of the property and that it is not entireties property. The deed or other instrument of title should be checked to see if the property is actually owned by the husband and wife.

(11) When land is owned by one party and improvements thereon or special rights (such as mineral, timber, quarry, waterpower, or similar rights) therein are owned by another party, the parties shall list their interests separately unless, in accordance with contractual relations between

them, both the land and the improvements and special rights are listed in the name of the owner of the land.

This subsection addresses the situation in which certain rights in land or improvements on land are owned by someone other than the owner of the fee. Mineral rights or separately owned buildings are two examples. Each separate right or improvement is to be listed in the name of the owner of the right or improvement unless the parties have agreed that the owner of the fee is to list both interests.[17]

> (12) If the person in whose name real property should be listed is unknown, or if title to real property is in dispute, the property shall be listed in the name of the occupant or, if there be no occupant, in the name of "unknown owner." Such a listing shall not affect the validity of the lien for taxes created by G.S. 105-355. When the name of the owner is later ascertained, the provisions of subsection (b), above, shall apply.

When, from an examination of the maps and land title records, the mapper and assessor are unable to determine the owner of a parcel of land, it is to be listed in the name of "unknown owner," unless there is an occupant of the land, then it is to be listed in the name of the occupant. "Occupant" here appears to be used in a broad sense, and does not mean that someone must be residing on the property. A person cutting timber on the property or cultivating the property, for example, would probably qualify as an occupant.

This subsection also directs how property is to be listed if the ownership is in dispute. Disputed ownership may occur when there are two apparent owners of record, or when the property has been listed in the name of "unknown owner" and a deed (usually a quitclaim deed) to the property is recorded, but the grantor is not in the chain of title, so far as the mapper can determine. Here, too, if there is an occupant of the property, the property is to be listed in his or her name.

If the owner of the property is subsequently ascertained, the listing is to be corrected in accordance with G.S. 105-302(b) (to be discussed in Section 303). If property has to be listed in the name of unknown owner for two successive listing periods and the taxes are unpaid, the taxing unit would be well advised to bring a foreclosure action against the property and sell it.[18] In many cases the thorough title search required in a foreclosure will identify the owner, and in others the search will show that the property does not exist as an independent parcel. In the event the property is sold under foreclosure, the purchaser becomes an identifiable owner.

> (13) Real property, owned under a time-sharing arrangement but managed by a homeowners association or other managing entity, shall be listed in the name of the managing entity.

This provision avoids the burdensome necessity of listing every time-share owner's interest, and instead requires the property, as a parcel, to be listed in the name of the homeowners' association or management organization.

§ 303. Changing or Correcting the Name of the Listing Owner

Introduction

Although one might expect that correcting tax abstracts and other records to reflect the property owner's name when a mistake has been made is a straightforward procedure, in fact it is not. The Machinery Act contains several overlapping provisions dealing with this matter. Although property mappers and assessors must be at some pains to discover who has authority to change the name of a listing owner and when such a change can be made, it ultimately makes very little difference as far as the taxes themselves are concerned. The tax lien attaches to the property every January 1, no matter who is listed as the owner, and the enforceability of that lien is unaffected by a mistake in the name of the listing owner.[19]

The discussion of this matter is divided according to the three time periods during which a change in the owner's name may be accomplished: before the first meeting of the board of equalization and review, during the time when the board of equalization and review is meeting, and after the board of equalization and review adjourns.

Before the First Meeting of the Board of Equalization and Review

G.S. 105-302(b) provides broadly that when property has been listed in the wrong name and the name of the owner is later ascertained, "the abstract and tax records shall be corrected to list the property in the name of the person in whose name it should have been listed. The corrected listing shall have the same force and effect as if the real property had been listed in the name of the proper person in the first instance." This statute does not state who is to make the correction, nor does it place any time limitations on when the correction can be made; that is, it does not state that beyond a certain time no correction can be made. No other statute expressly addresses the question of who may make the correction before the first meeting of the board of equalization and review, or even provides that a correction can be made before that meeting. Despite the absence of specific directions, it appears from the broad command of G.S. 105-302(b) that a correction can be made during that time, and, from the assessor's general control over the listing process,[20] it appears that the assessor is authorized to make the correction.

When the Board of Equalization and Review Is Meeting

From the date of the first meeting of the board of equalization and review until it adjourns,[21] the power to make corrections rests with the board.[22] The board may make the necessary corrections on its own initiative or at the request of any person.[23] This power is limited, however, to listings for the current year;[24] the board does not have authority to make corrections in listings for previous years.

After Adjournment of the Board of Equalization and Review

After the board of equalization and review adjourns, authority to change the name of the listing owner of property shifts to the board of county commissioners,[25] and the board may delegate this authority to the assessor.[26] Corrections under this statute [G.S. 105-325(a)(3)] are not limited to the current tax year, but may be made for any number of previous years. Also, the language of G.S. 105-302(b), indicating that a change shall have the same force and effect as though the property had been correctly listed in the first instance, is repeated.[27]

§ 304. Changing Appraised Values because of Errors in Quantity or Measurement

While this section does not deal with listing, and does not fit neatly in this chapter, the issues discussed are tax matters in which the mapper plays an important role. The best way to introduce the section is to give an example of a typical case in which the questions arise. A taxpayer has listed a parcel of property for ten years as containing 100 acres. The deed to the property, at the close of the description of the parcel, includes the following phrase, "containing 100 acres, more or less." There has never been a survey of the property, and both the property owner and the assessor have relied on the quantity stated in the deed as the amount of acreage to be listed. In 1994 the county completes a remapping of the entire county according to specifications of the state Land Records Management Program. When the map of this parcel is drawn and the acreage is calculated from the map, the quantity is shown to be ninety acres. Should the listed quantity be changed? What is the procedure for making such a change?

Changing Quantity on the Basis of a Mapping Project

The most reliable evidence of quantity is calculated from a proper survey of the property. If the quantity stated in a deed is not based on a survey, then it is probably based on the opinions of the parties to the deed, or of the parties to an antecedent instrument in the chain of title, or perhaps on the opinion of an adjacent landowner, or of a surveyor who made some rough calculations based on an inspection of the property. Legally, such a statement of quantity is not entitled to much weight.[28] In most cases, if the county's map is based on good aerial photographs, especially if it is based on orthophotographs, if the map was prepared according to state specifications, and if physical features such as roads or streams are located on the map, the quantity calculated from the map is more likely to be accurate than the quantity stated in the deed. Each case will depend on its particular facts, but if the property mapper believes the quantity calculated from the map is better evidence than the quantity stated in the deed and can explain why it is better evidence, the assessor should—on the basis of this evidence—change the listed quantity to conform to the map. The taxpayer may appeal this change to the board of equalization and review and to the Property Tax Commission. At each level of appeal the mapper must be prepared to explain and defend the change.

Changing Quantity in a Revaluation Year

If the assessor decides to change the quantity of listed property during a revaluation conducted pursuant to G.S. 105-286, the procedure is straightforward. The assessor makes the change as part of the reappraisal process and gives notice to the property owner. The owner then has the right of appeal, discussed in the subsection above. The change becomes effective on January 1 of the year the revaluation is effective,[29] and continues as the listing quantity until the county's next revaluation or until a change is required under G.S. 105-287.[30] For example, if, in the year following the revaluation, the taxpayer has the property surveyed and the quantity calculated from the survey (continuing with the example in the introduction) is ninety-five acres, the assessor would very likely change the listed quantity on the basis of the survey. Such a change would be made pursuant to G.S. 105-287 and would be effective as of January 1 of the year in which it was made; it would not be retroactive.[31]

Changing Quantity in a Nonrevaluation Year

G.S. 105-287 directs the assessor to change the appraisal of real property in a nonrevaluation year to

(1) Correct a clerical or mathematical error;
(2) Correct an appraisal error resulting from a misapplication of the schedules, standards, and rules used in the county's most recent general reappraisal or horizontal adjustment; or
(3) Recognize an increase or decrease in the value of the property resulting from a factor other than one listed in subsection (b).

The factors listed in subsection (b) are such things as general appreciation and depreciation and betterments such as painting and landscaping.

An appraisal change resulting from a change in quantity based on acreage calculated from a map should be made under subsection (3), "a factor other than one listed in subsection (b)." A change made under this statute is effective as of January 1 of the year in which it is made and is not retroactive.[32] In many cases in which the quantity, and therefore the appraisal, is reduced, the taxpayer will request that the reduction be carried back at least to the last revaluation and that he or she be given a release or refund of taxes, but under the statute this cannot be done. Moreover, the assessor may in many cases in which the quantity, and therefore the appraisal, is increased, wish to carry the increase back at least to the last revaluation and make a supplemental billing. This, too, is prohibited.

It should be emphasized that an appraisal change based on a change in quantity, of the sort discussed above, is not a discovery under G.S. 105-312, and because it is not a discovery, the assessor cannot reappraise the property for the current year, plus the five previous years. This is because the taxpayer has not made a substantial understatement of quantity or measurement but instead, has relied on the same information that was available to the assessor. Until better evidence of quantity becomes available, the taxpayer is entitled to rely on the quantity stated in the deed or other title document. Of course, cases may arise in which the disparity between the quantity stated in the deed and the actual quantity is so great—for example, when the deed calls for 50 acres and the actual quantity is 100 acres, and the taxpayer is an experienced landowner who regularly visited the property, that the assessor can assert that the taxpayer should have known there was an understatement and make a discovery of the unlisted acreage. But this will be a rare case, and the assessor must be prepared in such a case to convince the board of equalization and review and the Property Tax Commission that the taxpayer indeed should have known that an understatement was being made. In the ordinary case, the assessor should make the change under G.S. 105-287(a) and not under G.S. 105-312.

Notes

1. These are the statutory provisions governing the listing and assessing of property for ad valorem taxation and are found in Chapter 105, Subchapter II, of the N.C. General Statutes.

2. N.C. GEN. STAT. § 105-285(d). This does not mean that real property is reappraised every year; it is not. The appraisal schedule is established by Section 105-286 of the N.C. General Statutes (real property must be appraised at least octennially), and reappraisals of individual parcels are performed pursuant to Section 105-287. But each January 1, it becomes possible for the county assessor to change the appraisal of real property, and if a change is made it is effective as of January 1 of the year in which it was made and is not retroactive.

3. See Bemis Lumber Co. v. Graham County, 214 N.C. 167, 198 S.E. 843 (1938).

4. N.C. GEN. STAT. § 105-285(d).

5. Id. § 105-307.

6. Id.

7. Id. § 105-303(b) & S.L. 1999-297.

8. Id. §§ 105-303(b) & 105-302(a).

9. Id.

10. Id.

11. "Heirs" are the persons who take title to the property in the absence of a will; "devisees" are the persons who take title under the terms of a will.

12. See N.C. GEN. STAT. § 28A-13-3(a)(1).

13. Id. § 28A-13-3(c).

14. Id. § 28A-15-2(b).

15. See the discussion of these tenancies in Chapter I.

16. See the discussion of this form of ownership in Chapter I.

17. Under Section 105-355(a)(2) of the N.C. General Statutes, the taxes on the separate rights or improvements are a lien on the land.

18. All assessors must, upon request, furnish to the secretary of administration a report of properties listed in the name of unknown owner. N.C. GEN. STAT. § 105-302.1.

19. N.C. GEN. STAT. §§ 105-355(a) & 105-302(b).

20. *See id.* § 105-296(a).

21. The board's first meeting must be no earlier than the first Monday in April and no later than the first Monday in May. The board must adjourn by July 1, except to hear appeals that were requested before the announced adjournment date. N.C. GEN. STAT. § 105-322(e).

22. N.C. GEN. STAT. § 105-322(g)(1)b.

23. *Id.* § 105-322(g)(1).

24. *Id.*

25. *Id.* § 105-325(a)(3).

26. *Id.* § 105-325(b).

27. *Id.* § 105-325(a)(3)a.

28. *See* Tice v. Winchester, 225 N.C. 673, 36 S.E.2d 257 (1954).

29. N.C. GEN. STAT. §§ 105-285(d) & 105-286.

30. *Id.* § 105-285(d).

31. *Id.* § 105-287(c).

32. *Id.*

IV. Review Officer

§ 400. Introduction

This chapter deals with the duties of Review Officers,[1] many of whom are property mappers. Most maps and plats must be presented to and certified by a Review Officer before the register of deeds is allowed to record them. The presentation and recording procedures established by the applicable statutes contemplate that a map should be ready for recording when it is presented to a Review Officer; that is, that presentation to a Review Officer is the last step before recording the map in the register of deeds' office.

§ 401. Appointment and Qualifications

The board of commissioners of each county is responsible for designating, by resolution, one or more Review Officers in the county.[2] The Review Officer, or officers, should be designated by name, not by title. There is no requirement that a Review Officer be a county employee, so a board could designate a qualified municipal employee, if the municipal governing board consents to the designation. Persons designated should be experienced in mapping or land records management and "if reasonably feasible, be certified as a property mapper pursuant to G.S. 147-54.4."[3] If a Review Officer is to be allowed to delegate his or her authority to another person in the office, that authorization should be contained in the board's resolution. Such authority to delegate is a good idea because of the inevitable absences of the designated Review Officer for vacations, illnesses, and so forth. Someone must be available at all times to perform the review and certification functions. If, for example, Sherry Smith, the land records manager, is the designated Review Officer and she is authorized to delegate her authority, the resolution should say something like ". . . and she may delegate her duties as Review Officer to other qualified persons in her office." Then, if she has delegated her authority to her assistant, Dan Donaldson, and he signs a certificate in her absence, he would sign "Sherry Smith, Review Officer, by Dan Donaldson."

Any resolution designating a Review Officer, or officers, must be recorded in the register of deeds' office.[4] The register indexes these resolutions on the grantor index in the name of the Review Officer. A new resolution is required when a new Review Officer is appointed or a Review Officer resigns or retires.

§ 402. Review and Certification Duties

G.S. 47-30.2(b) states: "The Review Officer shall review expeditiously each map or plat required to be submitted to the Officer before the map or plat is presented to the register of deeds for recording. The Review Officer shall certify the map or plat if it complies with all statutory requirements for recording." The requirement of "expeditious" review means that the Review Officer must give the review and certification of a presented map a high priority, putting aside other work to accomplish the task in a timely manner. The Review Officer is to certify a map for recording "if it complies with all statutory requirements for recording." What are these requirements? They are in two categories: those intrinsic to the map, such as dimensions, regardless of the kind of map it is and whether it subdivides land and those regarding approvals of certain kinds of maps by government boards and agencies. The first category of requirements is contained in G.S. 47-30; the second category is contained in several other statutes.

Requirements of G.S. 47-30

Dimensions and Margin

Each register of deeds specifies the dimensions that a map must meet to be recorded in that office. A register may specify a size of 18 inches by 24 inches; a size of either 18 inches by 24 inches or 21 inches by 30 inches; a size of either 18 inches by 24 inches or 24 inches by 36 inches; or all three sizes.[5] The map must also have a minimum margin of 1 1/2 inches on the left side and 1/2 inch on the other sides.[6] The Review Officer must know the acceptable dimensions in the register's office and determine that each map presented is of the proper size and has the required margins that are clear of any printed material or drawings.

Reproducibility

G.S. 47-30(b) contains two separate requirements. The first is that each map presented for recording must be reproducible, that is, it must be capable of making legible copies. The second requirement is that it be on material that is archival, as defined by the American National Standards Institute. The Review Officer is expressly directed not to review maps to determine whether they are on material that is archival.[7] The Review Officer is, however, required to determine that the map is capable of making legible copies. Thus, the Review Officer must know the capacity and limitations of the recording equipment in the register's office and must review presented maps with this in mind. Typically, the Review Officer will be examining the material on which the map is made, the contrast between the lettering and lines and the background, the font size of any text, the boldness of lines, and the general legibility of the entire map. If any material on the original map is illegible or difficult to read, it is unlikely that the map will produce a legible copy.

Title Information

The Review Officer must ascertain that the information required in the map's title block by G.S. 47-30(c) is present. That information is the property designation (brief description); the name of the owner of the property; the location as to township, county, and state; the date the survey was made; the scale or scale ratio in words or figures and bar graph; and the name and address of the surveyor or surveying firm that prepared the map.

Surveyor's Signature, Certificate, and Seal

G.S. 47-30(d) requires the surveyor to make a certification in substantially the following form:

> I, _____, certify that this plat was drawn under my supervision from an actual survey made under my supervision (deed description recorded in Book ____, page ____, etc.) (other); that the boundaries not surveyed are clearly indicated as drawn from information found in Book ____, page ____; that the ratio of precision as calculated is 1: _____; that this plat was prepared in accordance with G.S. 47-30 as amended.
>
> Witness my original signature, registration number and seal this ____ day of _____.

The surveyor must sign this certificate with his or her original signature and affix his or her seal and registration number. The surveyor's signature is not required to be notarized. A surveyor may use a computer-generated seal but may not use a stick-on seal. The Review Officer must ascertain that all of these requirements have been met. A map that does not meet these requirements as to certificate, signature, and seal, but was prepared before October 1, 1997, and meets the certificate, signature, and seal requirements of G.S. 47-30 at the time it was prepared, should still be certified by the Review Officer, provided it meets all of the other requirements for certification.[8]

Land-Use Certification

G.S. 47-30(f)(11) requires each map to contain one of seven possible certifications by the surveyor regarding the use of the land covered by the map. The certification need not be exactly in the words of the statute, but it should hew closely to the statutory language. The seven possibilities are

> (f)(11)a. This survey creates a subdivision of land within the area of a county or municipality that has an ordinance that regulates parcels of land.
>
> (f)(11)b. This survey is located in a portion of a county or municipality that is unregulated as to an ordinance that regulates parcels of land.

(f)(11)c.1. This survey is of an existing parcel or parcels of land and does not create a new street or change an existing street.

(f)(11)c.2. This survey is of an existing building or other structure, or natural feature, such as a watercourse;

(f)(11)c.3. This survey is a control survey.

(f)(11)d. This survey is of another category, such as the recombination of existing parcels, a court-ordered survey, or other exception to the definition of a subdivision.

(f)(11)e. The information available to the surveyor is such that the surveyor is unable to make a determination to the best of the surveyor's professional ability as to provisions contained in G.S. 47-30(f)(11)a. through d.

The Review Officer must determine that one of these certifications is on the map. It is unlikely that the Review Officer will see certifications pursuant to (f)(11)b or c because maps with those certifications are exempt from review by the Review Officer, and the register of deeds will record such maps without the Review Officer's certification.[9]

Maps Prepared by a Deceased Surveyor

G.S. 47-30(h) directs the Review Officer to certify a map that was prepared by a surveyor who is deceased at the time the map is presented for recording, even though the map fails to meet one or more of the requirements of G.S. 47-30. The person presenting the map must, however, present evidence to the Review Officer that in fact the map was prepared by a deceased surveyor. This exemption from the requirements of G.S. 47-30 does not extend to the approval requirements discussed below. That is, for example, a subdivision plat prepared by a deceased surveyor must still meet the subdivision review and approval requirements.

Approvals Required by Other Statutes

Control Corners

Article 5A of Chapter 39 of the General Statutes (G.S. 39-32.1 through -32.4) requires that one or more permanent markers, known as "control corners," be designated in all subdivisions of land in which streets have been laid off and lots are offered for sale. G.S. 39-32.3 expressly provides that the control corners must be shown on the subdivision plat that is presented for recording before the Review Officer can certify it. This requirement of control corners applies whether or not the land being subdivided is covered by a city or county subdivision ordinance. The surveyor typically shows a control corner on a plat by drawing an arrow to the corner with the words "Control Corner."

Approval of Public Roads

G.S. 136-102.6 imposes certain requirements on subdivision plats that create new streets or roads or change existing streets or roads. When a landowner divides a tract or parcel into lots for residential sale or building development and creates a new street or changes an existing street, the landowner must record a plat of the subdivision with the register of deeds. Any new street or change in an existing street must be designated "public" or "private" on the plat. If a street is designated "public," subsections (d) and (c) provide that the Review Officer may not certify the plat for recording unless it has a certificate of approval from the local district engineer of the Division of Highways. If all of the streets are designated "private," no certificate of approval from the Division of Highways is required. The Review Officer's role is twofold. He or she must first ascertain that all new or changed streets on the plat are designated either "public" or "private." Then, if any street is designated "public," he or she must ascertain that a certificate of approval from the district engineer is affixed.

Approval of Subdivision Plats

G.S. 160A-373, for cities, and G.S. 153A-332, for counties, provide that when a city or county has adopted a subdivision ordinance, the Review Officer may not certify any subdivision plat for recording unless the plat has been approved by the appropriate city or county agency. In addition to this requirement of approval, there are certain situations in which "no approval required" must be entered on the map by the appropriate planning or other agency. If the surveyor makes a land-use certification pursuant to G.S. 47-30(f)(11)d. (survey is of another category) or e. (surveyor is unable to make a determination) and the applicable local ordinance requires either approval or a statement that no approval is required, then the Review Officer may not certify the plat unless the "no approval required" statement is on the plat.[10] Local subdivision ordinances should contain a requirement that the statement "no approval required" be entered on the plat if that is the case, and Review Officers should work with subdivision ordinance administrators to ensure that this is done. Several types of subdivision plats do not require approval,[11] and it is helpful to the Review Officer, the register of deeds, and users of the records if this is shown on the plat.

Water Supply Watershed Protection Ordinances

G.S. 143-214.5 requires cities and counties to adopt ordinances to protect public water supply watersheds in their jurisdictions. These ordinances may regulate the density of development in the watershed and require approval by a local government agency of any subdivision plat of land in the watershed. In cities and counties with subdivision ordinances, this approval will be part of the subdivision review and approval process,[12] and the Review Officer will simply look for the usual agency approval of the plat. But some cities and counties without subdivision ordinances may be required to regulate development in watersheds and approve subdivision plats of land in those watersheds. In such cases, may a local ordinance require subdivision plats to be submitted to the Review Officer before they are recorded and the Review Officer to determine that the agency responsible for enforcing the watershed protection ordinance has approved the plat? The answer appears to be "yes." Bear in mind that pursuant to G.S. 47-30.2, the Review Officer examines each map to determine that it complies with "all statutory requirements for recording." It is true that the watershed protection statute, G.S. 143-214.5, does not mention the Review Officer or require approval by the Review Officer, as do the other statutes discussed above, but G.S. 143-214.5 clearly requires local watershed protection ordinances to contain enforcement procedures and address development density issues. Therefore, it would seem that pursuant to the statutory commands of G.S. 143-214.5 a city or county without a subdivision ordinance could require subdivision plats to be presented to a Review Officer before recording and require the Review Officer to determine whether the appropriate agency approval had been given. Such requirements would be "statutory requirements for recording" within the meaning of G.S. 47-30.2. They are requirements that have their basis in statutory language.

Maps Attached to Other Instruments

Thus far the discussion regarding the Review Officer's responsibilities has been about free-standing maps, those presented for recording in the map and plat books and not as part of another instrument. Under certain conditions, however, a map may be recorded as an attachment to a deed or other instrument. Such maps must comply with one of two sets of requirements.

1. An attached map must be no larger than 8 1/2 inches by 14 inches. It must either contain a registered surveyor's original signature and seal or be a certified true copy of a previously recorded map that contains a surveyor's original signature and seal.[13] An attached map meeting these requirements must be presented to and certified by a Review Officer.[14]

2. An attached map not meeting the requirements of paragraph 1, above, may be recorded if it is not larger than 8 1/2 inches by 14 inches and contains the following statement: THIS MAP IS NOT A CERTIFIED SURVEY AND HAS NOT BEEN REVIEWED BY A LOCAL GOVERNMENT AGENCY FOR COMPLIANCE WITH ANY APPLICABLE LAND DEVELOPMENT REGULATIONS.[15] An attached map meeting these requirements is not required to be presented to a Review Officer before it is recorded.[16]

Review Officer's Certificate

After a Review Officer has determined that a map meets all statutory requirements for recording, the Review Officer must affix his or her certificate to the map, and the certificate is to be in substantially the following form:

State of North Carolina
County of _____

I, _____, Review Officer of _____ County, certify that the map or plat to which this certification is affixed meets all statutory requirements for recording.

_____   _____
Date   Review Officer

The Review Officer is not authorized to charge a fee for the certification.

§ 403. Exemptions

Not all maps are required to be certified by a Review Officer before the register of deeds is allowed to record them. The following categories of maps are exempt from certification by a Review Officer and may be recorded without such certification:

1. Maps which the surveyor has certified as to land use pursuant to G.S. 47-30(f)(11)b. or c.[17]
2. Maps attached to other instruments that meet the requirements of G.S. 47-30(n).[18]
3. Municipal annexation maps and municipal boundary maps.[19]
4. Highway right-of-way plans.[20]
5. Roadway corridor maps.[21]

Notes

1. The title "Review Officer" is capitalized in G.S. 47-30.3, and that convention is followed in this chapter.

2. N.C.Gen. Stat. § 47-30.2(a).

3. *Id.*

4. *Id.*

5. *Id.* § 47-30(a).

6. *Id.*

7. *Id.* § 47-30(g)(1).

8. *Id.* § 47-30(d).

9. *Id.* § 47-30.2(c)(1).

10. *Id.* § 47-30(f)(11), last paragraph.

11. *See id.* §§ 153A-335 and 160A-376 for exemptions.

12. *See id.* §§ 153A-332 and 160A-373 for subdivision approval requirements.

13. *Id.* § 47-30(m).

14. *See id.* § 47-30.2(c).

15. *Id.* § 47-30(n).

16. *Id.* § 47-30.2(c)(3).

17. *Id.* § 47-30.2(c)(1).

18. *Id.* § 47-30.2(c)(3).

19. *Id.* §§ 47-30.2(c)(2) and 47-30(j).

20. *Id.* §§ 47-30.2(c)(2) and 47-30(l).

21. *Id.*

Suggested Reading

Those interested in pursuing the study of property mapping, especially its legal aspects, may find the following publications helpful:

Curtis M. Brown, *Boundary Control and Legal Principles*, 2d ed. (New York: John Wiley & Sons, 1969).

William A. Campbell, *North Carolina Guidebook for Registers of Deeds*, 8th ed. (Chapel Hill, N.C.: Institute of Government, The University of North Carolina at Chapel Hill, 2000).

David M. Lawrence, *Local Government Property Transactions in North Carolina*, 2d ed. (Chapel Hill, N.C.: Institute of Government, The University of North Carolina at Chapel Hill, 2000).

David M. Lawrence, *Property Interests in North Carolina City Streets* (Chapel Hill, N.C.: Institute of Government, The University of North Carolina at Chapel Hill, 1985).

North Carolina Land Records Management Program, *Keys to the Modernization of County Land Records* [Raleigh, N.C.: Department of Administration (now in the Office of the Secretary of State), 1978].

North Carolina Land Records Management Program, *Technical Specifications for Base, Cadastral and Digital Mapping* [Raleigh, N.C.: Department of Natural Resources and Community Development (now in the Office of the Secretary of State), 1987].